www.providencebooks.net

Publisher Contact

Email:contact@providencebooks.net

Social media: facebook.com/providencebooks

Acknowledgements

The team at Providence Books would like to thank our friends, family, suppliers and customers for making our vision of creating the highest-quality books a reality. Thanks for purchasing and enjoy the quotes!

This page is intentionally left blank

This page is intentionally left blank

'Easter' is a movable event, calculated by the relative positions of sun and moon, an impossible way of fixing year by year the anniversary of a historical event, but a very natural and indeed inevitable way of calculating a solar festival. These changing dates do not point to the history of a man, but to the hero of a solar myth.

Annie Besant

A common religion is not possible for India, but a recognition of a common basis for all religions, and the growth of a liberal, tolerant spirit in religious matters, are possible.

Annie Besant

A myth is far truer than a history, for a history only gives a story of the shadows, whereas a myth gives a story of the substances that cast the shadows.

Annie Besant

A people can prosper under a very bad government and suffer under a very good one, if in the first case the local administration is effective and in the second it is inefficient.

Annie Besant

A prophet is always much wider than his followers, much more liberal than those who label themselves with his name.

Annie Besant

After death we live for some time in the astral world in the astral body used during our life on earth, and the more we learn to control and use it wisely now the better for us after death.

Annie Besant

All men die. You may say: 'Is that encouraging?' Surely yes, for when a man dies, his blunders, which are of the form, all die with him, but the things in him that are part of the life never die, although the form be broken.

Annie Besant

Among the various vernaculars that are spoken in different parts of India, there is one that stands out strongly from the rest, as that which is most widely known. It is Hindi. A man who knows Hindi can travel over India and find everywhere Hindi-speaking people.

Annie Besant

An accurate knowledge of the past of a country is necessary for everyone who would understand its present, and who desires to judge of its future.

Annie Besant

As a man may be born with a mathematical faculty, and by training that faculty year after year may immensely increase his mathematical capacity, so may a man be born with certain faculties within him, faculties belonging to the soul, which he can develop by training and by discipline.

Annie Besant

As civilisation advances, the deities lessen in number, the divine powers become concentrated more and more in one Being, and God rules over the whole earth, maketh the clouds his chariot, and reigns above the waterfloods as a king.

Annie Besant

As the heat of the coal differs from the coal itself, so do memory, perception, judgment, emotion, and will, differ from the brain which is the instrument of thought.

Annie Besant

At the solemn moment of death, every man, even when death is sudden, sees the whole of his past life marshalled before him, in its minutest details. For one short instant the personal becomes one with the individual and all-knowing ego. But this instant is enough to show to him the whole chain of causes which have been at work during his life.

Annie Besant

Beauty is no dead thing. It is the manifestation of God in nature. There is not one object in nature untouched by man that is not beautiful, for God's manifestation is beauty. It shines through all His works, and not only in those that may give pleasure to man.

Annie Besant

Better remain silent, better not even think, if you are not prepared to act.

Annie Besant

Britons are good, though often brutal, colonists where they come into relations with entirely uncivilized tribes whose past is so remote as to be forgotten. But they trample with their heavy boots over the sensitive, delicate susceptibilities of an ancient, highly civilized and cultured nation, such as India.

Annie Besant

Clairvoyants can see flashes of colour, constantly changing, in the aura that surrounds every person: each thought, each feeling, thus translating itself in the astral world, visible to the astral sight.

Annie Besant

Continents may break up, continents may emerge, but the human race is immortal in its origin and in its growth, and there is nothing to be afraid of, even if the foundations of the earth be moved.

Annie Besant

Death consists, indeed, in a repeated process of unrobing, or unsheathing. The immortal part of man shakes off from itself, one after the other, its outer casings, and - as the snake from its skin, the butterfly from its chrysalis - emerges from one after another, passing into a higher state of consciousness.

Annie Besant

Debating clubs among boys are very useful, not only as affording pleasant meetings and interesting discussions, but also as serving for training grounds for developing the knowledge and the qualities that are needed in public life.

Annie Besant

Empty-brained triflers who have never tried to think, who take their creed as they take their fashions, speak of atheism as the outcome of foul life and vicious desires.

Annie Besant

Every form, not being the whole, must, of necessity, be imperfect; less than the whole, it cannot be identical with the whole, and being less than the whole and, therefore, imperfect by itself, it shows imperfection as evil, and only the totality of a universe can mirror the image of God.

Annie Besant

Every person, every race, every nation, has its own particular keynote which it brings to the general chord of life and of humanity.

Annie Besant

Everyone knows the beautiful story of Abraham and the sacrifice of Isaac. How this noble father led his child to the slaughter; how Isaac meekly submitted; how the farce went on till the lad was bound and laid on the altar, and how God then stopped the murder, and blessed the intending murderer for his willingness to commit the crime.

Annie Besant

Evil is only imperfection, that which is not complete, which is becoming, but has not yet found its end.

Annie Besant

For centuries the leaders of Christian thought spoke of women as a necessary evil, and the greatest saints of the Church are those who despise women the most.

Annie Besant

I have ever been the queerest mixture of weakness and strength, and have paid heavily for the weakness.

Annie Besant

I often think that woman is more free in Islam than in Christianity. Woman is more protected by Islam than by the faith which preaches monogamy. In AI Quran the law about woman is juster and more liberal.

Annie Besant

I often think that woman is more free in Islam than in Christianity. Woman is more protected by Islam than by the faith which preaches monogamy.

Annie Besant

I was a wife and mother, blameless in moral life, with a deep sense of duty and a proud self-respect; it was while I was this that doubt struck me, and while I was in the guarded circle of the home, with no dream of outside work or outside liberty, that I lost all faith in Christianity.

Annie Besant

If we believe in a God at all, we must surely ascribe to him perfection of wisdom and perfection of goodness; we are then forced to conceive of Him - however strange it may sound to those who believe, not only without seeing but also without thinking - as without will, because He must always necessarily pursue the course which is wisest and best.

Annie Besant

In a deep metaphysical sense, all that is conditioned is illusory. All phenomena are literally 'appearances,' the outer masks in which the One Reality shows itself forth in our changing universe. The more 'material' and solid the appearance, the further is it from reality, and therefore the more illusory it is.

Annie Besant

In morals, theosophy builds its teachings on the unity, seeing in each form the expression of a common life, and therefore the fact that what injures one injures all. To do evil i.e., to throw poison into the life-blood of humanity, is a crime against the unity.

Annie Besant

India is a country in which every great religion finds a home.

Annie Besant

Isaiah is by far the finest and least objectionable of the seventeen prophets whose supposed productions form the latter part of the Old Testament. A distinctly higher moral tone appears in the writings called by his name, and this is especially noticeable in the 'Second Isaiah,' who wrote after the Babylonish captivity.

Annie Besant

Islam believes in many prophets, and Al Quran is nothing but a confirmation of the old Scriptures.

Annie Besant

It is not monogamy when there is one legal wife, and mistresses out of sight.

Annie Besant

It is the duty of the followers of Islam to spread through the civilised world, a knowledge of what Islam means - its spirit and message.

Annie Besant

Jeremiah is a most melancholy prophet. He wails from beginning to end; he is often childish, is rarely indecent, and although it may be blasphemy to say so, he and his 'Lamentations' are really not worth reading.

Annie Besant

Karma brings us ever back to rebirth, binds us to the wheel of births and deaths. Good Karma drags us back as relentlessly as bad, and the chain which is wrought out of our virtues holds as firmly and as closely as that forged from our vices.

Annie Besant

Let Indian history be set side by side with Europe history with what there is of the latter century by century and let us see whether India need blush at the comparison.

Annie Besant

Liberty is a great celestial Goddess, strong, beneficent, and austere, and she can never descend upon a nation by the shouting of crowds, nor by arguments of unbridled passion, nor by the hatred of class against class.

Annie Besant

Man is a spiritual intelligence, who has taken flesh with the object of gaining experience in worlds below the spiritual, in order that he may be able to master and to rule them, and in later ages take his place in the creative and directing hierarchies of the universe.

Annie Besant

Man is ever searching for the source whence he has come, searching for the life which is upwelling within him, immortal, nay, eternal and divine; and every religion is the answer from the Universal Spirit to the seeking spirits of men that came forth from Him.

Annie Besant

Matter is, in its constituent elements, the same as spirit; existence is one, however manifold in its phenomena; life is one, however multiform in its evolution.

Annie Besant

Men are at every stage of evolution, from the most barbarous to the most developed; men are found of lofty intelligence, but also of the most unevolved mentality; in one place there is a highly developed and complex civilisation, in another a crude and simple polity.

Annie Besant

Muhammadan law in its relation to women, is a pattern to European law. Look back to the history of Islam, and you will find that women have often taken leading places - on the throne, in the battle-field, in politics, in literature, poetry, etc.

Annie Besant

My first serious attempts at writing were made in 1868, and I took up two very different lines of composition; I wrote some short stories of a very flimsy type, and also a work of a much more ambitious character, 'The Lives of the Black Letter Saints.'

Annie Besant

My own life in India, since I came to it in 1893 to make it my home, has been devoted to one purpose, to give back to India her ancient freedom.

Annie Besant

Never yet was a nation born that did not begin in the spirit, pass to the heart and the mind, and then take an outer form in the world of men.

Annie Besant

No durable things are built on violent passion. Nature grows her plants in silence and in darkness, and only when they have become strong do they put their heads above the ground.

Annie Besant

No philosophy, no religion, has ever brought so glad a message to the world as this good news of Atheism.

Annie Besant

Nothing but an imperious intellectual and moral necessity can drive into doubt a religious mind, for it is as though an earthquake shook the foundations of the soul, and the very being quivers and sways under the shock.

Annie Besant

One of the great advantages of cremation - apart from all sanitary conditions - lies in the swift restoration to Mother Nature of the material elements composing the physical and astral corpses, brought about by the burning.

Annie Besant

Premonitions, presentiments, the sensing of unseen presences and many allied experiences are due to the activity of the astral body and its reaction on the physical; their ever-increasing frequency is merely the result of its evolution among educated people.

Annie Besant

Quick condemnation of all that is not ours, of views with which we disagree, of ideas that do not attract us, is the sign of a narrow mind, of an uncultivated intelligence. Bigotry is always ignorant, and the wise boy, who will become the wise man, tries to understand and to see the truth in ideas with which he does not agree.

Annie Besant

Refusal to believe until proof is given is a rational position; denial of all outside of our own limited experience is absurd.

Annie Besant

Representative institutions are as much a part of the true Briton as his language and his literature.

Annie Besant

Science regards man as an aggregation of atoms temporarily united by a mysterious force called the life-principle. To the materialist, the only difference between a living and a dead body is that in the one case that force is active, in the other latent.

Annie Besant

Socialism is the ideal state, but it can never be achieved while man is so selfish.

Annie Besant

Strange indeed would it be if all the space around us be empty, mere waste void, and the inhabitants of Earth the only forms in which intelligence could clothe itself.

Annie Besant

Sun-worship and pure forms of nature-worship were, in their day, noble religions, highly allegorical but full of profound truth and knowledge.

Annie Besant

That is the true definition of sin; when knowing right you do the lower, ah, then you sin. Where there is no knowledge, sin is not present.

Annie Besant

The Buddha over and over again spoke clearly and definitely on post-mortem states - as in his conversation with Vasetta.

Annie Besant

The Roman Catholic Church, had it captured me, as it nearly did, would have sent me on some mission of danger and sacrifice and utilised me as a martyr; the Church established by law transformed me into an unbeliever and an antagonist.

Annie Besant

The birth of science rang the death-knell of an arbitrary and constantly interposing Supreme Power.

Annie Besant

The body is never more alive than when it is dead; but it is alive in its units, and dead in its totality; alive as a congeries, dead as an organism.

Annie Besant

The destruction of India's village system was the greatest of England's blunders.

Annie Besant

The divine life is the spirit in everything that exists, from the atom to the archangel; the grain of dust could not be were God absent from it; the loftiest seraph is but a spark from the eternal fire, which is God. Sharers in one life all form one brotherhood. The immanence of God, the solidarity of man, such are the basic truths of theosophy.

Annie Besant

The essence of religion is the knowledge of God which is eternal life. That and nothing less than that is religion. Everything else is on the surface, is superfluous save for the needs of men.

Annie Besant

The generous wish to share with all what is precious, to spread broadcast priceless truths, to shut out none from the illumination of true knowledge, has resulted in a zeal without discretion that has vulgarised Christianity, and has presented its teachings in a form that often repels the heart and alienates the intellect.

Annie Besant

The highest Hindu intellectual training was based on the practice of yoga, and produced, as its fruit, those marvellous philosophical systems, the six Darshanas and the Brahma Sutras, which are still the delight of scholars and the inspiration of occultists and mystics.

Annie Besant

The human body is constantly undergoing a process of decay and of reconstruction. First builded into the astral form in the womb of the mother, it is built up continually by the insetting of fresh materials. With every moment tiny molecules are passing away from it; with every moment tiny molecules are streaming into it.

Annie Besant

The idea of reverence for God is transmitted from parent to child, it is educated into an abnormal development, and thus almost indefinitely strengthened, but yet it does appear to me that the bent to worship is an integral part of man's nature.

Annie Besant

The idea that Buddhism denies what is called in the West 'individual immortality' is a mistake, so far as the Buddhist scriptures are concerned.

Annie Besant

The mental body, like the astral, varies much in different people; it is composed of coarser or of finer matter, according to the needs of the more or less unfolded consciousness connected with it. In the educated it is active and well-defined; in the undeveloped it is cloudy and inchoate.

Annie Besant

The orthodox believers in God are divided into two camps, one of which maintains that the existence of God is as demonstrable as any mathematical proposition, while the other asserts that his existence is not demonstrable to the intellect.

Annie Besant

The soul grows by reincarnation in bodies provided by nature, more complex, more powerful, as the soul unfolds greater and greater faculties. And so the soul climbs upward into the light eternal. And there is no fear for any child of man, for inevitably he climbs towards God.

Annie Besant

The sunlight ranges over the universe, and at incarnation we step out of it into the twilight of the body, and see but dimly during the period of our incarceration; at death we step out of the prison again into the sunlight, and are nearer to the reality.

Annie Besant

The true basis of morality is utility; that is, the adaptation of our actions to the promotion of the general welfare and happiness; the endeavour so to rule our lives that we may serve and bless mankind.

Annie Besant

The worlds in which man is evolving as he treads the circle of births and deaths are three: the physical world, the astral or intermediate world, the mental or heavenly world.

Annie Besant

Theosophy has no code of morals, being itself the embodiment of the highest morality; it presents to its students the highest moral teachings of all religions, gathering the most fragrant blossoms from the gardens of the world-faiths.

Annie Besant

Theosophy tries to bridge the gulf between Buddhism and Christianity by pointing to the fundamental spiritual truths on which both religions are built, and by winning people to regard the Buddha and the Christ as fellow-laborers, and not as rivals.

Annie Besant

There can be no wise politics without thought beforehand.

Annie Besant

There is a charm in making a stew, to the unaccustomed cook, from the excitement of wondering what the result will be, and whether any flavour save that of onions will survive the competition in the mixture.

Annie Besant

There is far more misunderstanding of Islam than there is, I think, of the other religions of the world. So many things are said of it by those who do not belong to that faith.

Annie Besant

There is much, of course, in the exclusive claims of Christianity which make it hostile to other faiths.

Annie Besant

This Old Testament - containing error, folly, absurdity and immorality - is by English statute law declared to be of divine authority, a blasphemy - if there were anyone to be blasphemed - blacker and more insolent than any word ever written or penned by the most hotheaded Freethinker.

Annie Besant

To me in my childhood, elves and fairies of all sorts were very real things, and my dolls were as really children as I was myself a child.

Annie Besant

We have no right to pick out all that is noblest and fairest in man, to project these qualities into space, and to call them God. We only thus create an ideal figure, a purified, ennobled, 'magnified' Man.

Annie Besant

We learn much during our sleep, and the knowledge thus gained slowly filters into the physical brain, and is occasionally impressed upon it as a vivid and illuminative dream.

Annie Besant

We were an ill-matched pair, my husband and I, from the very outset; he, with very high ideas of a husband's authority and a wife's submission, holding strongly to the 'master-in-my-own-house theory,' thinking much of the details of home arrangements, precise, methodical, easily angered and with difficulty appeased.

Annie Besant

What is a philosophy? It Is an answer satisfactory to the reason to all the great problems of life. That is what is meant by philosophy. It must satisfy the reason, and it must show the unity underlying the endless diversity of the facts that science observes.

Annie Besant

What is the constitution of the universe? The universe is the manifestation of the divine thought; the thought of God embodies itself in the thought-forms that we call worlds.

Annie Besant

What is the essence of theosophy? It is the fact that man, being himself divine, can know the divinity whose life he shares. As an inevitable corollary to this supreme truth comes the fact of the brotherhood of man.

Annie Besant

What, after all, is the object of education? To train the body in health, vigor and grace, so that it may express the emotions in beauty and the mind with accuracy and strength.

Annie Besant

You should always take a religion at its best and not at its worst, from its highest teachings and not from the lowest practices of some of its adherents.

Annie Besant

This page is intentionally left blank

This page is intentionally left blank

This page is intentionally left blank

This page is intentionally left blank

This page is intentionally left blank